A BUSINESS APPROACH TO BLUEBERRY FARMING

Complete Entrepreneurial Step By Step Guide To Blueberry Garden From Scratch

ZHURI HART

DISCLAIMER

This book is intended to provide general information and insights on adopting a business approach to farming. The content within is based on the author's knowledge and experiences up to the date of publication. It is essential to recognize that the field of agriculture is dynamic, influenced by various factors such as market conditions, climate, and regulatory changes.

Readers are advised to conduct thorough research, seek professional advice, and consider their unique circumstances before implementing any strategies or practices discussed in this book. The author and publisher disclaim any responsibility for the accuracy, completeness, or suitability of the information provided. The book is not a substitute for professional advice, and the author and publisher shall not be liable for any damages or losses arising from the use or reliance on the information presented herein.

Individual results may vary, and success in farming enterprises is contingent upon numerous variables. The author encourages readers to consult with relevant experts, agricultural extension services, and legal or financial professionals to tailor strategies to their specific needs and local conditions.

This book is not intended to be a comprehensive guide to all aspects of farming, and readers should exercise their judgment and discretion in applying the principles discussed. The author and publisher do not endorse any specific products, services, or companies mentioned in this book unless explicitly stated.

By reading this book, the reader acknowledges and accepts the inherent uncertainties in agricultural endeavors and agrees to use the information at their own risk.

TABLE OF CONTENTS

ABOUT THE BOOK

"A Business Approach to Blueberry Farming," a book that offers a thorough overview of the commercial side of blueberry production, fills a significant gap in the agricultural literature. Because of their many uses and health advantages, blueberries have become more and more popular, which has made growing them a lucrative endeavor.

This book is significant because it fills a gap that exists between conventional farming manuals and the unique requirements of business owners starting or growing in the blueberry sector.

The book establishes the scene in the first section by outlining the history and importance of blueberry production. The stated objectives provide readers with a road map to navigate the contents of the book, and the identification of the target audience guarantees that the information applies to both beginning farmers and seasoned farmers looking to expand their businesses.

The comprehension of blueberries part explores the nuances of blueberry kinds, development needs, and the life cycle, providing crucial information for productive cultivation. The reader is better prepared for the upcoming chapters by having a firm understanding of the biology and ecology of blueberries.

An essential part that aids farmers in navigating the intricacies of supply and demand is the market analysis portion. Through an examination of market trends, opportunities, and the competitive environment, readers acquire critical insights necessary to make well-informed decisions on their farming businesses.

The planning section of the book, which covers equipment selection, farm layout, site selection, and financial planning, demonstrates its applicability. These factors, which are frequently disregarded in general agricultural guides, are essential for starting a successful blueberry farm.

The methods used for cultivation, harvesting, and handling blueberries after harvest provide farmers with additional guidance on the operational parts of the business. The book's dedication to making sure that the produced blueberries fulfill industry standards and boost market competitiveness is further demonstrated by the inclusion of quality control and certification procedures.

The following chapters, which cover marketing, finance, and sustainability, provide a comprehensive guide to operating a profitable blueberry farm. A thorough company plan must include building a brand, comprehending sales channels, and putting sustainable principles into action.

"A Business Approach to Blueberry Farming" is an invaluable tool for anyone looking to build and run a profitable company in the fast-paced and cutthroat blueberry market in addition to effectively cultivating blueberries.

CHAPTER ONE

BLUEBERRY FARMING INTRODUCTION

THE HISTORY AND SIGNIFICANCE OF BLUEBERRY AGRICULTURE

The cultivation of blueberries has become an important agricultural endeavor, adding to the agricultural landscape on a worldwide scale. The history of blueberry farming spans several centuries, and the first people to appreciate the potential of these little, tasty berries were Native American tribes. Blueberries are now a popular and adaptable fruit in the contemporary market thanks to their evolution from wild gathering to organized farming practices over time.

Beyond its historical origins, blueberry farming has become increasingly significant due to the berries' considerable health advantages. The abundance of antioxidants found in blueberries is widely known, and this contributes significantly to the promotion of general health.

Due to their high vitamin and mineral content, blueberries are a great complement to a diet that is well-balanced. The importance of blueberry production in the agricultural industry is fueled by the rising demand for blueberries as a result of expanding consumer knowledge of the berries' health advantages.

COMPREHENDING BLUEBERRIES

To truly comprehend blueberries, one must explore the complexities of their development, growth, and farming. The Vaccinium genus of plants includes blueberry plants, which are distinguished by their deciduous nature. They need regular upkeep and care during the growing season because they do well in acidic soil. Blueberry plants go through several stages in their life cycle, from flowering to fruiting, and each stage needs particular environmental conditions to flourish as best it can.

Understanding the particular difficulties and needs that come with growing blueberries is another aspect of cultivating this crop. The application of efficient pest management techniques is required due to the vulnerability of blueberry plants to specific pests and diseases. Furthermore, blueberries are pH-sensitive, thus maintaining the acidity levels necessary for their growth requires careful consideration of soil additives. Farmers must have a thorough awareness of these elements to guarantee a successful blueberry harvest.

DIFFERENT TYPES OF BLUEBERRIES

Varieties of blueberries add to the industry's diversity in blueberry growing. There are numerous varieties of blueberries, and each has unique qualities like as size, flavor, and climate tolerance. Common blueberry cultivars include rabbiteye, lowbush, and highbush, each with special benefits for growing. The right blueberry variety should be chosen based on several characteristics, including the intended application (export, processing, or fresh consumption), soil requirements, and climate.

The history and significance of blueberry growing underscore its continued relevance in the current era of health-conscious customer preferences. Farmers must grasp the complexities of blueberry growth and cultivation to successfully manage the difficulties this crop presents. The variety of blueberry cultivars highlights how flexible and adaptable blueberry farming is, which helps to explain why blueberry cultivation has remained significant in the agricultural industry.

CHAPTER TWO

GROWTH CONDITIONS

CONDITIONS OF THE SOIL

The state of the soil has a major impact on how plants grow and develop. Aeration, water retention, and the availability of vital nutrients are all directly impacted by the structure and makeup of the soil. Certain plants have preferences for particular types of soil, and elements like pH, texture, and organic matter concentration can affect a plant's ability to flourish. Certain plants, including those that prefer acidic soil, do well in such conditions, but others could need loamy or well-draining soils.

The microbial activity in the rhizosphere is influenced by soil conditions, which also have an impact on nutrient uptake and general plant health. For effective farming and long-term growth, soil conditions must be understood and optimized.

CLIMATE-RELATED ISSUES

Because they determine the climatic conditions that are prevalent in a certain area, climate factors are essential to the growth requirements of plants. The three main variables that affect plant growth are temperature, humidity, and precipitation amounts. Temperature requirements for germination, growth, and flowering differ amongst plants. While some plants are suited to temperate or desert regions, others flourish in tropical settings that are consistently warm and humid. The duration of the growing season and the kinds of crops that can be grown in a specific location are also influenced by the climate. It is crucial to modify cultivation techniques to regional climate trends to maximize plant yield and guarantee development.

GROWTH STAGES AND THE LIFE CYCLE

Plants go through several various phases in their life cycle and growth stages, each with its own set of requirements. Stages including seed germination, vegetative growth, blooming, fruiting, and senescence are commonly included in the life cycle. Plants require certain nutrients and environmental conditions at these phases. For instance, plants need more nitrogen during the vegetative phase to develop their leaves, and they also need more potassium and phosphorus during the blooming and fruiting stages to expand their reproductive organs to their full potential.

Timing cultivation techniques like fertilizer, irrigation, and pest control to match the plant's changing needs during its development requires an understanding of the life cycle and growth stages.

Knowledge of the life cycle and growth stages of plants, as well as soil and climate factors, are critical to the success of plant growth. Cultivators can establish an environment that supports strong and healthy plant development by carefully evaluating and manipulating these parameters. To guarantee that the plants being produced receive the right nutrients, water, and environmental conditions at every stage of their life cycle, it is imperative to customize cultivation techniques to meet their unique requirements. Whether used in large-scale farming operations or smaller-scale gardening projects, this all-encompassing strategy supports efficient and sustainable agricultural methods.

CHAPTER THREE

EXAMINATION OF THE MARKET

THE MARKET FOR BLUEBERRIES

There is a noticeable increase in the market demand for blueberries due to several reasons that increase customer preference for them. Growing evidence points to blueberries as a superfood full of health-promoting chemicals and antioxidants. Due to customers' increasing health consciousness and need for nutrient-dense foods, blueberries are in high demand. The fact that blueberries are versatile and can be eaten frozen, fresh, or processed into jams and juices increases their appeal to a wider range of consumers.

OPPORTUNITIES AND MARKET TRENDS

There is a change in the market toward consuming more fresh and organic blueberries. Customers are growing more discriminating and looking for goods that suit their tastes for natural and ecologically sourced materials. Producers now have the chance to stand out from the competition and take advantage of the expanding market demand for organic blueberries thanks to this trend.

The popularity of internet grocery shopping platforms has also made it simpler for people to obtain blueberries, making it more convenient for them to be included in their diets.

Moreover, consumer preferences are changing quickly in the blueberry sector, and there is a discernible demand for products infused with blueberries in a variety of market groups. Yogurts, cereals, and snacks with blueberry flavors have grown in popularity, demonstrating how versatile blueberries are in terms of food applications.

This trend encourages businesses to look for novel and inventive ways to include blueberries in a wide range of consumer items, which presents the potential for creativity and product development.

COMPETITIVE ENVIRONMENT

Different firms are fighting for market share in the blueberry industry within the competitive landscape. Large- and small-scale producers alike are arranging themselves tactically to fulfill the growing demand. Geographical variables are important; areas with climates conducive to blueberry growth see a rise in competition from both domestic and foreign businesses.

The productivity and efficiency of blueberry farms are also being impacted by developments in agricultural technology and growing techniques, which are raising the competitiveness of market players.

The worldwide aspect of the blueberry business, with nations like the US, Canada, Chile, and Spain emerging as major participants in blueberry production and export, further shapes the competitive environment. Global trade dynamics and alliances can have an impact on blueberry availability and cost, as well as market trends. Companies are carefully aligning themselves to overcome hurdles and capitalize on emerging possibilities as the market continues to change. They are stressing elements like quality, sustainability, and innovation to stand out in a competitive market.

CHAPTER FOUR

ORGANIZING YOUR FARM TO GROW BLUEBERRIES

SITE CHOOSING

Choosing the ideal location for your blueberry farm is an essential first step toward making the business profitable. Blueberries grow best in acidic, well-drained soils that range in pH from 4.0 to 5.5. To evaluate the pH, nitrogen levels, and soil makeup of the possible site, perform a comprehensive soil analysis. Blueberry plants require full sun exposure, so pick a spot that receives enough of it.

In addition, take into account elements that could affect the general health of the blueberry bushes, such as the availability of water, the slope, and the closeness to other crops. Selecting a location for your blueberry plants that allow for enough air circulation will help shield them from disease and encourage healthy growth.

FARM DESIGN AND LAYOUT

The next crucial stage is to design a functional and effective farm layout after you've chosen a suitable location. Think about the rows, spaces, and accessibility of the arrangement. Planting blueberries requires a sufficient amount of space to promote airflow and facilitate harvesting. To guarantee constant moisture levels, especially during the growing season, plan for effective irrigation systems. Provide access points and walkways so that workers and equipment may move around the farm with ease. Putting into practice a well-thought-out design that considers the land's natural contours can also aid in water drainage and avert possible problems like water logging.

INFRASTRUCTURE AND EQUIPMENT

Purchasing the appropriate equipment is crucial to your blueberry farm's profitability. Tractors for cultivating and plowing, specialist blueberry harvesters, and irrigation systems are examples of equipment that may be required. Make sure the equipment you have is in good working order and appropriate for the size of your farm. Installing a weather station can help you make more accurate management decisions by tracking temperature, humidity, and precipitation. Establish infrastructure as well, including sheds for packing blueberries, a small office for administrative work, and storage spaces for gathering blueberries. Sufficient infrastructure enhances your blueberry farm's overall productivity in addition to supporting day-to-day activities.

FINANCIAL PLANNING AND BUDGETING

Making a thorough financial strategy and budget is crucial to your blueberry farm's long-term viability and profitability. Commence by calculating the expenses related to equipment purchase or rental, planting supplies, irrigation systems, site preparation, and continuing upkeep. Include the cost of manpower, fertilizers, and pest control techniques in your operational budget. The amount of time it takes for blueberry bushes to reach maturity and start bearing fruit should also be taken into account since this will affect your initial outlay and anticipated returns. Create a marketing plan to sell your blueberries, whether you choose to distribute them wholesale, sell them directly to customers, or sell them at local markets. Review and modify your financial strategy regularly as your blueberry farm grows and the market changes. Achieving financial planning and budgetary efficiency is crucial for managing possibilities and obstacles in the ever-changing agricultural sector.

CHAPTER FIVE

AGRICULTURAL METHODS

PLANTING METHODS

One of the most important factors in the success of growing operations is planting techniques. Various techniques are used by farmers based on the crop type, climate, and soil conditions. Whereas transplanting entails growing seedlings apart before moving them to the field, direct seeding involves putting seeds straight into the ground. Every strategy has benefits and drawbacks. While transplanting offers greater control over plant spacing and early growth, direct sowing is more economical but may have issues with uneven spacing and poor germination.

Aside from the manner of planting, other important considerations are timing, spacing, and seed depth. An ideal seedling location guarantees maximum germination, and suitable seed spacing facilitates effective solar exposure and nutrient uptake. Climate has an impact on when to plant because crops might be sensitive to changes in temperature and amount of daylight. An effective cultivation cycle is mostly dependent on the establishment and early growth of crops, which is greatly aided by effective planting procedures.

SYSTEMS OF IRRIGATION

Maximizing yields and maintaining crop development depend on effective irrigation. Different irrigation techniques are used according to crop needs, soil type, and water availability. Conventional techniques like surface irrigation—which includes flood and furrow irrigation as well—involve saturating the field with water. Although these techniques are easy to use and inexpensive, they may lead to uneven distribution and water waste.

Water application precision is increased using modern irrigation methods like sprinkler and drip irrigation. By delivering water straight to the root zone, drip irrigation reduces water loss and evaporation. Sprinkler systems ensure even coverage by dispersing water through overhead sprays. Several variables, including crop variety, climate, and budgetary constraints, influence the irrigation system selection. Using effective irrigation techniques helps to increase crop output and health while also conserving water.

METHODS OF FERTILIZATION

One of the most important aspects of cultivation techniques is fertilization, which gives plants the nutrients they need to grow and develop. Crop rotation, cover crops, and organic and inorganic fertilizers are just a few of the fertilizing techniques used by farmers. Compost and manure are examples of organic fertilizers that improve soil structure and nutrient content while encouraging microbial activity. Conversely, inorganic fertilizers provide exact nutritional ratios that enable farmers to target particular deficits.

Growing specific plants to increase soil fertility, stop erosion, and control weeds is known as cover cropping. Crop rotation is a technique that breaks the cycles of pests and diseases while preserving the health of the soil. It involves rotating crops in a particular order. Sustainable farming depends on balancing nutrient inputs according to crop requirements and soil analysis. Using a customized fertilization plan helps maximize yield overall, promote crop vigor, and improve soil fertility.

MANAGEMENT OF PESTS AND DISEASES

Managing diseases and pests well is essential to productive farming operations. To protect crops against pests and diseases, farmers use a variety of techniques, such as chemical treatments, cultural practices, and biological management. The use of natural predators or parasites to manage pest populations is known as biological control. Cultural methods can assist lower the incidence of illness.

Examples include timely pruning, keeping ideal plant spacing, and rotating crops properly.

When all other options have been exhausted, chemical interventions like fungicides and insecticides are frequently utilized to contain serious disease and pest outbreaks. Integrated pest management (IPM) and sustainable techniques, on the other hand, try to reduce dependency on pesticides. To maintain a resilient and balanced environment, integrated pest management (IPM) employs a range of measures, such as monitoring insect populations, utilizing resistant crop types, and putting biological controls in place.

To effectively manage pests and diseases, regular scouting, early discovery, and prompt intervention are essential. Long-term resilience against possible threats is also aided by enhancing biodiversity in and around fields and teaching farmers sustainable practices. For farmed crops to remain healthy and productive, thorough pest and disease management strategies must be put into place.

CHAPTER SIX

HARVESTING AND HANDLING AFTER HARVEST

IDEAL TIME FOR HARVESTING

A crucial component of agricultural techniques that has a big impact on crop output and quality is optimal harvesting time. To maximize the nutritional value and overall market worth of the crop, harvesting at the appropriate time is crucial. Harvesting times vary from crop to crop and depend on several variables, including weather patterns, markers of crop maturity, and the planned use of the harvested goods. To ensure the crop achieves its top quality, farmers generally use visual assessments, technology techniques, and expertise to determine the best time to harvest.

TECHNIQUES FOR HARVESTING

Harvesting techniques are essential for preserving crop integrity and reducing losses after harvest. The type of crop, its physical properties, and the intended final product all influence the harvesting method selection. Manual harvesting, mechanical harvesting, and selective harvesting are common methods of harvesting. For fragile fruits and vegetables, hand harvesting is frequently preferable; nevertheless, mechanized methods are effective for large-scale production. To guarantee consistent quality, selective harvesting entails selecting only fully developed or ripe crops.

CLASSIFYING AND EVALUATING

Among the crucial post-harvest handling procedures that increase the marketability and acceptability of agricultural products by consumers are sorting and grading. Sorting entails dividing the gathered produce into different categories according to standards like size, color, and quality. On the other hand, grading gives the sorted produce a quality categorization that frequently affects pricing and market placement. Grading and sorting work together to produce a uniform and aesthetically pleasing product that satisfies customer demands and makes for effective market distribution.

TRANSPORTATION AND STORAGE

The post-harvest supply chain's storage and transportation systems have a direct impact on the quality and shelf life of agricultural products. To slow down the natural deterioration processes, proper storage facilities are designed to maintain ideal conditions, including temperature, humidity, and ventilation. Selecting the right mode of transportation is also essential to avoid damage while en route. From the field to the customer, cold storage, refrigerated vehicles, and other cutting-edge technologies are essential for maintaining the freshness and nutritional content of produced vegetables.

The success of agricultural operations depends on having a thorough awareness of the following topics: optimal harvesting time, harvesting techniques, sorting and grading, storage, and transportation. Farmers may cut post-harvest losses, improve the overall quality of their produce, and strengthen the resilience of the food supply chain by implementing effective and well-managed procedures in these areas.

CHAPTER SEVEN

CERTIFICATION AND QUALITY ASSURANCE

HIGHEST LEVELS OF QUALITY

Benchmarks or requirements known as quality standards are established to make sure that goods and services fulfill particular needs for dependability, performance, and safety. To create a shared knowledge of quality expectations, organizations, trade associations, or regulatory agencies create these standards.

Businesses need to adhere to quality standards to obtain a competitive advantage, improve customer happiness, and meet regulatory requirements. ISO 9001 for quality management, ISO 14001 for environmental management, and ISO 45001 for occupational health and safety are a few examples of internationally recognized quality standards.

PROCEDURES FOR CERTIFICATION

The use of certification processes is essential for confirming that set quality standards are being met. A methodical assessment of a process, service, or product against preset standards is required for certification. Usually, independent third-party certification agencies conduct this assessment on behalf of the organization applying for certification. The certification procedure consists of evaluations, on-site audits, and documentation reviews to make sure the company satisfies the required quality standards. Obtaining certification shows a dedication to quality and gives stakeholders, consumers, and government agencies peace of mind that the good or service satisfies the requirements.

THE BEST METHODS FOR ENSURING QUALITY

A variety of tactics and approaches are included in best practices for quality assurance to guarantee that procedures always produce results of the highest caliber. These procedures are intended to reduce errors, boost productivity, and encourage ongoing development. Total Quality Management (TQM), which places a strong emphasis on staff involvement, customer happiness, and continuous process improvement, is one commonly used strategy. Using key performance indicators (KPIs) to track and measure quality metrics is another useful technique. Other crucial best practices include creating a strong quality management system, carrying out frequent audits, and encouraging a culture of quality consciousness among staff members.

A complete quality management system must include both certification and quality control. Activities and procedures used to keep an eye on and regulate the consistency and conformance of goods or services throughout manufacturing or delivery are referred to as quality control. The goal of this procedure is to find and fix flaws or departures from accepted standards of quality. However, external validation of an organization's adherence to these criteria is provided through certification. When combined, these procedures help to raise consumer trust, lower risks, and improve the company's reputation overall.

Upholding and verifying quality standards are essential components of guaranteeing that goods and services satisfy consumer demands and legal mandates. Following quality assurance best practices aids businesses in creating a culture of ongoing development and client satisfaction. Adopting quality standards and certification procedures is crucial for remaining competitive and proving a dedication to excellence as industries change.

CHAPTER EIGHT

STRATEGIES FOR MARKETING AND SALES

CREATING YOUR BRAND FOR BLUEBERRIES

In a market where there is competition, developing a powerful and enduring brand for your blueberries is essential. It takes more than simply creating a visually appealing logo or package to complete the process; you also need to have a thorough understanding of your target market, positioning in the market, and USPs. Start by determining the salient features and characteristics that make your blueberries unique from competitors' offerings. This could involve elements like unique kinds, sustainable farming methods, or better flavor. Include these components in your branding plan to establish a unique identity that appeals to customers.

Think about your brand's visual components, such as the packaging, color palette, and logo design. The idea is to convey the freshness and quality of your blueberries through a unified, aesthetically pleasing design. Employ powerful narrative techniques in your branding to tell the tale of your farm while highlighting openness and sincerity. Emphasize any distinctive farming practices, cherished family customs, or community service that gives your brand personality. Maintaining consistency across the whole brand experience—from packaging to internet presence—helps create a trustworthy and identifiable brand.

CHANNELS OF SALES

To maximize revenue streams and reach a wider audience, diversifying sales channels is imperative. Investigate direct-to-consumer methods like farmers' markets, internet platforms, or farm stands in addition to conventional retail stores. Opportunities for direct sales provide you the chance to interact more personally with customers, highlight the superior quality of your products, and get quick feedback.

To increase your reach through wholesale channels, interact with nearby distributors, supermarkets, and grocery shops. Building trusting connections with these partners can result in regular orders and more exposure on shop shelves. Use e-commerce platforms to capitalize on the expanding trend of grocery shopping online, which offers customers convenience and creates new revenue streams.

Additionally, think about collaborating with cafes, restaurants, and food service providers to include your blueberries on their menus. Working together with chefs and culinary influencers can help your brand become more visible and generate demand in the food service industry. Having a broad range of sales channels in place not only boosts income but also protects your company from shifts in the market and customer preferences.

DEVELOPING CONNECTIONS WITH PURCHASERS

The connections you make with customers through a variety of media are critical to the success of your blueberry business. Emphasize openness and communication to foster loyalty and trust. Engage with customers regularly to learn about their needs, preferences, and comments. When it comes to improving your goods and services to better satisfy consumer needs, this knowledge is priceless.

Developing relationships with buyers requires networking. Attend industry events, trade exhibitions, and networking gatherings to interact with possible buyers and keep informed about market developments. Establishing a personal connection can frequently make a major impact on a buyer's decision-making process. Share the story of your brand, the quality of your blueberries, and the unique value proposition you offer.

Provide excellent customer service by addressing inquiries promptly and efficiently handling any issues that may arise. Consider offering incentives or exclusive deals to repeat buyers, fostering loyalty, and encouraging long-term partnerships.

CHAPTER NINE

FINANCIAL MANAGEMENT

COST ANALYSIS

Cost Analysis is a fundamental aspect of financial management that involves the systematic examination and evaluation of the various costs associated with a business operation.

This process aims to provide insights into the allocation of resources, identify areas for cost reduction, and enhance overall efficiency. Cost analysis encompasses both direct costs, such as raw materials and labor, and indirect costs, including overhead expenses.

By understanding the components of costs and their impact on the overall financial performance, organizations can make informed decisions to optimize resource utilization and improve profitability.

REVENUE PROJECTIONS

Revenue Projections play a pivotal role in financial management as they involve estimating future income streams based on various factors, such as market trends, customer behavior, and economic conditions. Accurate revenue projections are essential for strategic planning, budgeting, and decision-making. Organizations employ different forecasting techniques, including quantitative models and qualitative assessments, to project revenues. Financial managers must consider potential risks and uncertainties when developing revenue projections to ensure realistic and achievable financial goals. Regularly revisiting and updating these projections enables businesses to adapt to changing market conditions and make timely adjustments to their financial strategies.

RISK MANAGEMENT

Risk Management is a critical function in financial management that involves identifying, assessing, and mitigating potential threats to an organization's financial well-being. Financial risks can arise from various sources, including market volatility, credit defaults, operational failures, and external economic factors.

Through a comprehensive risk management process, businesses can develop strategies to minimize the impact of adverse events and capitalize on opportunities. This involves implementing risk identification tools, risk assessment methodologies, and risk mitigation strategies. By proactively managing risks, financial managers can protect the organization's financial health, enhance decision-making, and contribute to long-term sustainability.

Cost Analysis, Revenue Projections, and Risk Management are interconnected concepts that collectively contribute to effective financial management. Cost analysis aids in understanding resource allocation and optimizing efficiency, revenue projections facilitate strategic planning and goal-setting, and risk management ensures the protection of financial assets in the face of uncertainties. Together, these concepts form a robust framework for organizations to navigate the complex financial landscape, make informed decisions, and achieve sustainable financial success.

CHAPTER TEN

SUSTAINABILITY PRACTICES

ENVIRONMENTAL CONSIDERATIONS

In the realm of sustainability practices, environmental considerations play a pivotal role in shaping responsible and ethical business operations. Companies across various industries, including agriculture, are increasingly recognizing the significance of minimizing their ecological footprint. In the context of blueberry farming, several key environmental considerations come to the forefront.

One crucial aspect is soil health and conservation. Sustainable blueberry farming emphasizes practices that promote soil fertility and reduce erosion. Techniques such as cover cropping and crop rotation not only enhance the quality of the soil but also contribute to long-term agricultural sustainability. Additionally, the prudent use of water resources is paramount.

Implementing efficient irrigation systems and water conservation measures helps mitigate the environmental impact associated with intensive agricultural practices.

Biodiversity conservation is another vital component of environmentally conscious blueberry farming. Maintaining natural habitats around farms, preserving wildlife corridors, and avoiding the use of harmful pesticides are integral steps toward safeguarding biodiversity.

By embracing organic farming methods and integrated pest management, blueberry farmers can contribute to the overall health of ecosystems and protect pollinators crucial for crop production.

COMMUNITY ENGAGEMENT

Community engagement is an essential facet of sustainable practices, fostering collaboration and shared responsibility between businesses and the local populace. In the context of blueberry farming, community engagement goes beyond the farm gates to encompass a range of interactions and partnerships that benefit both the farming operation and the surrounding community.

Firstly, transparent communication and active dialogue with local communities are crucial. By keeping residents informed about farming practices, potential environmental impacts, and the benefits derived from sustainable approaches, blueberry farmers can build trust and foster a positive relationship with their neighbors. In some cases, community input can even contribute to refining farming practices to align better with local needs and concerns.

Furthermore, supporting local economies through employment opportunities and sourcing materials locally is integral to sustainable community engagement. Blueberry farms can play a role in creating jobs and contributing to the economic well-being of the communities they operate in. Additionally, collaborating with local schools, organizations, and government entities can lead to mutually beneficial initiatives, such as educational programs, infrastructure development, and community events.

SOCIAL RESPONSIBILITY IN BLUEBERRY FARMING

Social responsibility in blueberry farming involves a commitment to ethical labor practices, fair treatment of workers, and overall contributions to the well-being of the communities where farming operations are based. This encompasses aspects ranging from workers' rights to community development initiatives.

Ensuring fair wages, safe working conditions, and access to essential amenities are fundamental components of social responsibility in blueberry farming. Fair labor practices not only benefit the workers directly but also contribute to the overall sustainability of the industry. This includes providing opportunities for training and skill development, thereby enhancing the livelihoods of those involved in the farming process.

Additionally, social responsibility extends to broader community development efforts. Blueberry farms can actively contribute to local schools, healthcare facilities, and infrastructure projects, improving the overall quality of life for community members. By engaging in philanthropic initiatives and supporting social programs, blueberry farmers can play a significant role in fostering social cohesion and well-being in the areas they operate.